Published by Lexilore Publications
Printed in UK by The Cromwell Press
ISBN 0-9550189-1-9

Lexilore Publications
Peveral Walk
Basingstoke
RG22 6QA

# Acknowledgements

Thanks must go to the following persons for their assistance directly or indirectly in compiling this book and general input; instructors Barry Michael, Marty Lau, Gary Wang and Nigel Chivers, also to Juli Norris, Paul Flint and the rest of the printing team.

# About the author

Martial Arts have been a way of life for Guy Edwards from a very early age. He is a former student and instructor under Grand Master (Victor) Kan Wah Chit (nicknamed 'the king of Chi Sau' for his peerless Sticking Arm ability), one of the top five students of the late Great Master Yip Man.

Guys' interest in Martial Arts extends beyond the physical realms, he also enjoys the spiritual dimensions and esotorics of the Chinese, Indonesian and Filipino fighting systems.

# Contents

# Introduction

Welcome. In my last book "Wing Chun Kung Fu - a Southern Chinese Boxing System" we explored all the quintessential fundamentals for building a firm base. These included the solo practice of positions within the first form, various ways of conditioning and two man co-ordination and sensitivity drills of the Single Sticking Arm, also some examples of simultaneous attack and defence.

In this book I will endeavor to show you the next all important phase of the Wing Chun system - The Double Sticking Arms. Each time I write I want to bring something new to the table because I fully realise that there are already many journals existing on this style.

The particular version of Sticking Arms I am detailing are of the "Classical or Traditional" variety, not one of the modern contemparies in vast circulation. Please bear in mind the late Great Grand Master Yip Man already modified Wing Chun in the first place by removing what he thought to be "outdated or theatrical", in other words he made it less flowery and more functional for the era and location.

In saying that it is well known Yip Man taught differently at various periods and according to the size, intelligence and capability of each student. This is why we have both subtle and vast differences in the standards of Yip Mans' students.

It's fair enough to adopt the notion of " take it and make it your own", but if everyone started doing this we would begin to lose sight of the original system. Therefore the more people start adding their own stuff the more diluted it becomes, just like when you add too much water to a glass when making orange squash.

The book you are about to read is divided into three main sections namely; Sticking Arms (the bulk of which), Searching for the Bridge (the 2nd form of Wing Chun) and lastly the Fighting Applications.

Please note that learning Sticking Arms requires you to have a training partner or better still a variety of training partners ie. tall, small, slender, powerfully built, fast, strong, conditioned and knowledgeable. There are some solo drills you can perform, but only so much, so find a training partner and really take your time with the basics.

Guy Edwards

# PART 1
# TACTICS & PRINCIPLES

# Sticking Arm Tactics

**FORWARD ENERGY FLOW** - Maintain a constant forward pressing force while in contact with your opponent.

**USE NO ARTIFICIAL STRENGTH** - Don't use any kind of wasted muscle power or brute force. By doing so you will expend all your energy very quickly and become exhausted in a very short time.

**STICK WHENEVER POSSIBLE** - Try to stick closely to your opponent's limbs when at the right distance. If separated try to close the gap quickly and safely to regain your sticking flow.

**GAIN GROUND WHENEVER POSSIBLE** - Edge forward with your footwork confusing and disrupting your opponent's posture and spoiling their momentum

**USE TACTILE FEELING** - Tune yourself into the subtle changes occurring when engaged in sticking arms. Continuously feel the vibrations and develop a high sense of tactile awareness.

**USE YOUR EYESIGHT** - Pick out any of your opponent's intentions by looking indirectly and using your side or peripheral vision.

**USE YOUR HEARING & SENSE OF SMELL** - If you can, listen carefully for the sound of your opponent's movement (ie. rubbing of clothing) even use your sense of smell to identify your opponent's strike coming into range.

**ORGANISE CORRECT ALIGNMENT** - When your positions are thoroughly organised you become more powerful and more difficult for your opponent to attack.

**CHECK YOUR REFERENCE POINTS** - While practicing with your opponent go slowly, pausing, checking, stopping, re-adjusting and organising your reference points.

**AVOID ANTICIPATION** - Don't expect your opponent's movement, try to empty your mind and react as you feel or see, so you can respond accordingly with the appropriate counter attack.

**CONSERVE YOUR ENERGY** - Pace yourself and don't get flustered when being attacked. Keep your breathing pattern as normal as you can.

**STAY AS RELAXED AS POSSIBLE** - Although there is much to remember you must adopt a sensation of calmness, even comfor,t when in engaged in sticking. Doing so will enhance spontaneity.

**AVOID CHEAPSHOTS** - Sticking Arms training is like a game of chess in that it requires concentration and tactics. Crude speed hits spoil the concept of what you are striving to achieve, more importantly it can prove to being a highly dangerous mistake when up against a seasoned opponent.

**CONSTANT CHANGE** - Don't create any comfort zones in your practice. Expect everchanging actions and disruptions. Cope with what ever comes when it comes.

**COUNTER ATTACK WHENEVER POSSIBLE** - Respond immediately like a shadow to your opponent's actions. Try to counter attack as automatically as you can, taking advantage of everything.

# Dexterity Enhancement

In Wing Chun Sticking Arms we are engaging a responsive tactile set of motions, which is why co-ordination and sensitivity has to be trained. We do this by trying to improve our overall dexterity. Have you ever met anyone who was ambidextrous, totally comfortable with using either their left or right hand? For some people it's a gift that just comes naturally, but in saying that it can be achieved to a high level with the right kind of practice. Aside from plenty of drilling the Single Sticking Arm exercises you can enhance your hand to eye co-ordination by practicing some dexterity games. Always try to improve your weaker arm so do extra on your left arm if you're right handed and vice versa.

- Practice writing with your weaker arm (solo)

- Practice juggling with different objects (solo)

- Catching different objects (two man)

- Paper / Scissors / Stone (two man)

- Pat-a-cake (two man)

- Learn to play musical instruments (both sides)

- Play the card game 'Snap' at speed with your weaker arm (two man)

These are just a small example of the variety of co-ordination attributes that you can 'play' with to complement your own Sticking Arms training. I'm sure you can think of others.

# Auto Response

   To enhance your Sticking Arms ability you must use the "economy of motion" so that you can respond to an oncoming attack as it happens. Receiving, assessing and responding must be automatic. You want to condense any thinking time down to a bare minimum with no hesitations, and how do we do this?....through practice, but not just any kind it must be the correct practice.

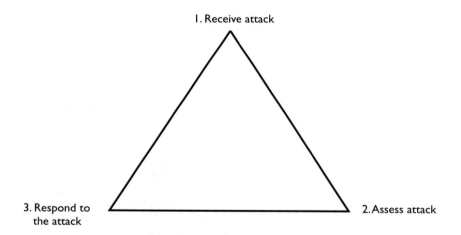

# Distance and Positioning

CLOSE  MID  LONG

Three main ranges

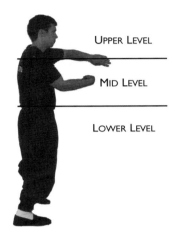

UPPER LEVEL

MID LEVEL

LOWER LEVEL

Three main levels

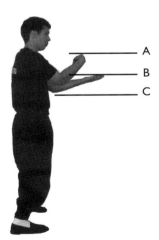

A
B
C

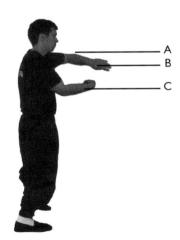

A
B
C

A. Fok Sau must not go above this point

B. Tang Sau fingertips point towards the opponent's solar plexus.

C. Tang Sau acts as the fixed elbow.

A. Bong Sau elbow higher than wrist.

B. Bong Sau fingertips point towards the opponents solar plexus.

C. Fok Sau must not go below this point and acts as the fixed elbow.

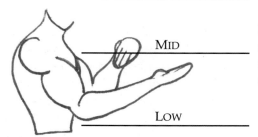

HIGH

MID

LOW

Range - The three levels of range can differ according to the height and build of your opponent.

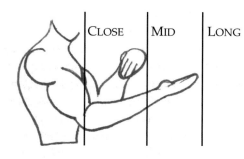

CLOSE    MID    LONG

Distance - Similary there are three levels of distance which can also fluctuate according to your opponent's arm reach.

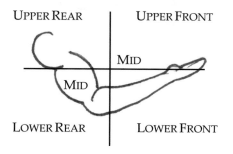

UPPER REAR          UPPER FRONT

MID

MID

LOWER REAR          LOWER FRONT

Neutral - When training with an opponent of the same height and build use the neutral posture which comprises of a mid range and mid distance base.

# About Breathing

Due to the physical exertion involved with Sticking Arms practice and the raising of the heartbeat, the breathing pattern can become a little erratic. Try your best to overcome this by trying to breathe as smoothly and evenly as you possibly can. Breathe steadily in and out through your nose keeping your teeth clinched gently together and your tongue pressing against the upper palate of your mouth on the pressure point. This will help to keep your mouth moist and stop it drying up, it also plays a major role in circulating your energy.

# Return to Sender

The more you practice "Counter for Counter" drills the more natural they become. Your hand to eye co-ordination can improve vastly in a short amount of time (with the right practice obviously) making it easier to introduce new motions of various complexities. After a while you will feel confident enough to 'let go' if you like. This is where you can alternate at will continually feeling the opponent's motions and most importantly, integrating with them. Your tactile awareness and counter reflex will have to cope with the sudden changes of the broken rhythm or disengagement and this is where the theory of "a strike can become a block" and "a block can become a strike" can apply.

# PART 2
## PREPARATION

# Vital Preparation

Practice the basics thoroughly before you begin to move on to the Sticking Arms training and don't take shortcuts. By now you should have acquired a reasonably good working knowledge of the basics ie. a solid stance, strong turning powers, well conditioned forearms. You should be familiar with the positions of attack and defence coupled with the terminology for them either in English, Cantonese or Mandarin Chinese (or even a combination of all!)

If you haven't studied at least the rudimentary basics then you need to do so. Just remember a larger opponent with more strength will have no advantage against a smaller opponent who has spent much time developing the Gung Lik (building energies) and all the hard work that you cannot see visually.

From my early personal experience of Sticking Arms I can tell you that those who spent lengthy amounts of time repeating and honing the basics over and over were amongst the most difficult to attack. In some cases their stance would be so strong that you couldn't even make them budge! As for their arm positions, they were so well organised it was near impossible to intercept or attack them, meanwhile their own attacks seemed so powerful, effortless and precise that I would be sent reeling backwards uncontrollably! Another annoying point I would notice was how utterly at ease they appeared under these stressful conditions, whereas I would begin to tire and get flustered very quickly. So the importance of basics should never be ignored and people progress at different speeds depending on if they can "grab the concept", understand and absorb the teachings that are being imparted. There is no set time limit. You also have to take into consideration how frequently a person is training but it is generally suggested that you spend approximately one year on the basics including the first form "Siu Nim Tau".

# The Build Up

Start your training with a warm up, please don't neglect it as Sticking Arms practice works every little muscle group and can be very demanding. Perform some soft stretching followed by a little cardio (optional) to raise the heart rate. Now go through all the basics such as the stance, centre punching, inside and outside punching, palm, side palm, front kick & side kick, turning punch, twisting punch, forward and backward shuffle etc. After these begin the "Siu Nim Tau" (Little Idea) first form of Wing Chun. Take your time with the third section, sometimes referred to as the "Pray thrice to Buddha", concentrating on calm deep breathing accompanied by the single forearm slow dynamic tension. Collecting power and charging the human battery. After this section you will release the energy and by the end of the form you will be fully energised and ready for the two man drills.

With your opponent begin to drill some arm conditioning, followed by "Paak Sau" (slapping arm) against Centre punching, "Tang Dar" (palm up arm with strike), against outside punches, "Garn Dar" (cultivating arm with strike), "Lop Dar" (grabbing arm with strike) and so on. Okay, after a few good worthy repetitions you move on to the "Dan Chi Sau" (single Sticking Arm) exercises gradually building up to the "Lok Sau" (rolling arms) phase.

*Author's note:*
*The concept of warming up with the basics to gradually introducing the more intermediate actions of Sticking Arms is merely a recommended suggestion. Under no circumstances am I dictating how the practitioner should set his or her training program.*

# Framework

Use plenty of framework only. By that I mean the basic systematic rolling, feeling your opponent's every motion using a continuous forward (not downward!) force. You should be constantly aware of not just your opponent's actions but also your own throughout, concentrating and analysing everything in a smooth but deliberate sequence. After completing the rolling cycle several times refresh yourself by switching and changing to start the rolling cycle vice versa. Increase switching and changing motion as you become more comfortable, let's say every two or three roll cycles now, setting your mind and limbs into continuous change.

From there you can drill some basic "give and take" exercises from a stationary position improving your arm dexterity and co-ordination. Once you have practiced this for a few minutes you can introduce some footwork subtly pushing and pulling your opponent. You should be practicing plenty of "Yin Yang" motions such as the moving forward with attack versus moving backward with defence. Remember lots and lots of framework so don't skip the main course to get to the peaches and cream!....practice plenty of rolling only at first and don't forget the opponent with the "Tang Sau" (palm up arm) will control the next roll cycle for practice sake.

# So Much to Remember

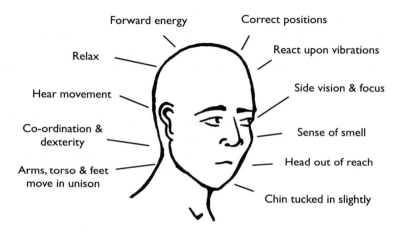

Forward energy

Correct positions

Relax

React upon vibrations

Hear movement

Side vision & focus

Co-ordination & dexterity

Sense of smell

Arms, torso & feet move in unison

Head out of reach

Chin tucked in slightly

Like I mentioned before, practice slowly when learning new skills. Dissect and analyse everything. Blocks and strikes can be performed fast and dynamically, but always use pauses in between so you can make any necessary adjustments. In the beginning it can be mind boggling trying to remember all relative positions and ideas so don't be put off.

The worst thing you could do is relentlessly attack a seasoned opponent before you know how to deal with the potential consequences, remember this old adage "fools go rushing in" you don't want to get a punch on the nose or a kick to the groin, so train carefully.

# Single Sticking Arms

Before you begin to learn Poon / Lok Sau - Rolling Arms then the next Suerng Chi Sau - Double Sticking Arms, you need to develop some grounding in the Dan Chi Sau - Single Sticking Arm. Trying to progress without learning the exercise could be counter-productive as the Single Sticking gives you all the fundamental keys, such as tactile awareness, tempo and momentum, co-ordination etc.

I have already included the drill in my previous book "Wing Chun Kung Fu - a southern chinese boxing system", so I won't repeat it here. Developing good Dan Chi Sau has no time restriction but should be taught to the student gradually, move by move over several months.

*Author's note: A little known fact is that the Single Sticking Arm was not part of the original Wing Chun system but was created by the late Great Grand Master Yip Man to enable his students to comprehend the Double Sticking Arms more efficiently.*

# PART 3
# ROLLING ARMS

# Rolling Arms Preparation

1a) Right Tang Sau - Palm up arm with upper left Fok Sau - Controlling arm (neutral)

1b) Roll cycle one: Right Bong Sau - Wing arm with lower left Fok Sau

2a) Roll cycle two: Right Tang Sau with upper left Fok Sau

2b) Roll cycle one: Right Bong Sau - Wing arm with lower left Fok Sau

# Side View

1a) Right Tang Sau just off the 45° angle while the Fok Sau is set at no higher than the chest (neutral)

1b) Roll cycle one: Right Bong Sau elbow raised with wrist set a little lower than chest height. Lower left Fok Sau just off the 45° angle.

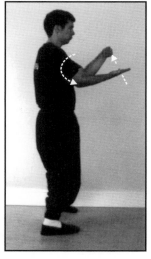

2a) Roll cycle two: Right Tang Sau with left Fok Sau (neutral)

2b) Roll cycle two: Right Bong Sau elbow raised with wrist set a little lower than chest height. Lower left Fok Sau just off 45° angle.

# Levels of Pressure

The levels of pressure when learning Sticking Arms can fluctuate immensely. A knowledgeable - "Sifu" (teacher)guides the student through the Yin/Yang forces over the period of months or years. Firstly the student will learn the basic positions very lightly, later on in time gradual forward pressure will become prevalent. This will be repeated more and more untill the student can cope with very heavy forward pressure, then finally the student will be guided back to the light forward pressure or "Bik Ging". The reason for this often overlooked method of learning Sticking Arms is to be able to deal with the strength of an opponent. It's not a wrestling match , that's true, but if you've only known the light Sticking Arms how will you handle a larger more aggressive opponent? So the chief point to this is to develop your 'iron bridges' (arms) so they don't collapse under stress and the way to develop this is through this Gung Lik (effort energy) type of training.

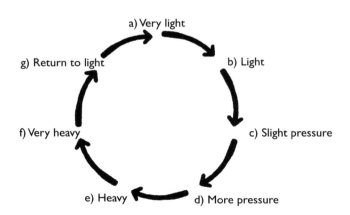

This diagram demonstrates the several modes of continuous forward pressing energy experienced in StickingArms training.

# The Neutral Leads

One of the prominent "rules of play" when practicing Double (or Single) Sticking is the concept of the person in the Tang Sau / Fok Sau (neutral) position takes the lead to the next motion Bong Sau / Fok Sau exchange. This is repeated in a vice versa fashion, passing back and fourth the control between the two opponents.

# Timing, Pace and Momentum

When starting off the rolling cycle it pays to do the actual movements swiftly, but using small pauses in between. This pausing action is especially applicable to the controlling (neutral) Tang Sau / Fok Sau position. In time with experience the practitioners can increase the speed and momentum of their Sticking Arms to a faster pace.

# Peripheral Vision

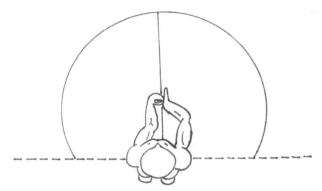

Try gazing indirectly at your training partner once you have grasped a good working knowledge of the Sticking Arms basics.

In the beginning you'll have to use plenty of 'eagle eye' vision to feed and register both your own and your opponent's motions. But in time with practice this will become more subtle to the point where you can use peripheral or side vision to analyse the situation. Casting the eyesight over your opponent's shoulder can actually help to feel the partner's intentions rather than looking directly at them.

# Rolling Arms (Two Man)

1a) Partner A assumes the Tang Sau / Fok Sau position. Partner B links on with the Bong Sau / Fok Sau position.

1b) Roll cycle one: Partner A leads from the neutral position into the Bong Sau / Fok Sau position.

2a) Roll cycle two: Partner B controls the motion by changing from neutral back to the Bong Sau / Fok Sau

2b) Roll cycle three: Partner A leads from the neutral position again into the Bong Sau / Fok Sau.

3a) Roll cycle four: Partner B controls again by changing back from neutral to the Bong Sau / Fok Sau position

3b) Roll cycle five: Partner A once again switches back to the Bong Sau / Fok Sau position.
And so on...

# Switching & Changing

Once you have trained the framework of the Rolling Arms to a satisfactory level or in other words you have practised the drill until it becomes natural, you are then ready to start introducing the basic switching and changing positions.

Maintaining the tactile feeling when switching and changing is vital, you have to bear in mind that you can be vulnerable to attacks when doing so. Switching and changing is helpful in the fact that you can alternate to the other arm cycles efficiently and thus refreshing the arm that's done the difficult work.

There are a few different ways to switch and change, practise these motions frequently (every four or five cycles) paying special attention to smoothness of application so as not to interrupt the flow. Remember feel and stick!

Switching is simple to do:

☐ The moment your partner initiates the switch you must follow.

☐ Keep the gap when changing tightly secure allowing possible opening or leakages.

☐ When your partner employs the Huen Sau - Circling Arm to change you automatically switch to a Tang Sau - Palm Up arm and so on...

# PART 4
# STICKING ARMS

# Chi Sau Drill

(Yin / Defence) Wu Sau - Praying Arm combined with reverse step.

1) From the last roll cycle pause the arms at the Bong Sau / Fok Sau position.

2a) Retract left foot employing an inward semi circle combined with a Wu Sau while maintaining a fixed Bong Sau / Fok Sau position.

2b) Keeping the upper body stable, edge backward slightly with the lead foot to close the gap of your stance.

3) Once the pressure is off move forward immediately returning to the original position. Do this in one smooth motion adjusting the Wu Sau back to a Fok Sau and ready to begin the next cycle.

# Side View

1) Pause in the Bong Sau / Fok Sau position.

2a) Turn your right Fok Sau to a Wu Sau while stepping backward

2b) Stabilise your upper body as you retract the lead foot a little.

3) Return to the first position quickly.

## Tips

☐ Make sure your Bong Sau is solid and doesn't collapse.

☐ Use your footwork in quick short shuffles rather than wading strides. Maintain more weight on the rear leg.

☐ Keep Wu Sau elbow in tight next to ribcage and fingers turned upwards as far as possible. Blocking downward slightly not backwards.

☐ Move body as one unit keeping head from arm's reach.

☐ Keep the shoulders and torso parallel.

(Yang / Attack) Tang Sau - Palm up entrance combined with foreward step

1) From the neutral position pause and get ready to move forward.

2a) Step forward employing an inward semi-circle while maintaining the fixed arm position.

2b) Keeping the upper body stable, edge forward slightly with the lead foot to close the gap of your stance.

3) Once the pressure is off move backward immediately returning to the original position. Do this in one smooth motion adjusting the Wu Sau back to a Fok Sau and ready to begin the next cycle.

# Side View

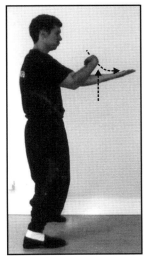

1) Pause in the Tang Sau / Fok Sau neutral position.

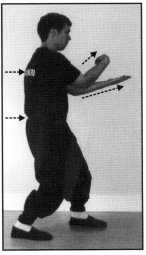

2a) Move the left foot forward so it corresponds with the left Tang Sau.

2b) Stabilise your upper body as you move forward with rear foot a little.

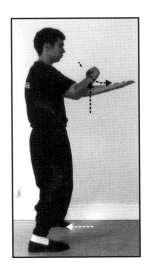

3) Return to the first neutral position quickly.

## Tips

☐ Maintain the correct angles for neutral position.

☐ Keep the gap between your TangSau and your Fok Sau tight. Apply slight tension to elbow area.

☐ Use your footwork in quick short shuffles rather than wading strides. Maintain more weight on the rear leg.

☐ When advancing with forward step blast through the middle.

☐ Move body as one unit keeping head from arm's reach.

☐ Keep the shoulders and torso parallel.

# The Yin /Yang Cycle

Once you have thoroughly practiced both the Yin (defending) and Yang (attacking) modes you need to connect them.

Partner A steps backwards and combines a Wu Sau to Partner B forward attack with Palm Strike.

# Keep a Safe Distance.

One of the most common mistakes a practitioner can make is not keeping the right distance. Keep your head out of the way and the Bong Sau arm position at the right distance at all times.

Partner A checks the distance between Partner B's eyes by waving a potential finger strike.

# It's Only a Drill

Just remember the training exercises I am describing in this book are the key fundamentals. It's up to you to develop them through plenty of practice and hard work. All the drills included might take you a long time to perform correctly, but they are essential to any serious progression.

The book could contain two thousand pages of Chi Sau drills for various scenarios but there's absolutely no reason for this. It's all very well thinking to yourself "Yeah right....well if you tried to do this, I would do that....(turn to the side instead of stepping back or punch you on the nose when moving forward)". But this is missing the object and beauty of the Sticking Arms. Like I've mentioned before we are only interested in the essence, once you have learned this you will be able to expand on it.

# Sticking Arms in Other Styles

Firstly Sticking Arms training is a very ancient practice and can be found in many different styles of fighting arts from every region of the world. In fact the "sticking" concept can be found in pretty much every system from India to France! And the reason why?.... because it works! Physical confrontation is all about gaining control of your opponents and in a close quarter situation it's vital to have some kind of tactile control on your attacker's limbs. Once you've absorbed the art of "sticking" you'll find it indispensable as you'll be able to apply it to everything, hands, feet, weapons etc; the theory is the same.

It's true that Wing Chun employs quite a range of complex movements within its Sticking Arms and the angles and positions are very specific indeed. No matter how unique Chi Sau seems the true essence is exactly the same as all the other kinds of Sticking Arms training. In Tai Chi you have "Pushing Arms" also "Waving Arms" in some styles of Kung Fu or in the Filipino martial arts they have "Hubbud Lubbud" and Indonesian martial arts they have "Kilap", the list goes on. Although there are obviously some subtle differences the general principals of using Sticking motions, counter for counter motions and application of forward energy are totally universal.

There are some schools of Wing Chun that only practice the sticking arms training and leave out all of the hand and weaponary forms. these schools are sometimes referred to as the "Wing Chun Lite". Another group of people integrating Chi Sau into their syllabus are the practitioners of "Jeet Kune Do" a conceptional fighting system developed by the late Bruce Lee. In fact with the ever growing popularity of mixed martial arts and cross training more and more groups are adding to the Wing Chun version of Sticking Arms to their regime.

# Modern Variations

1. Fok Sau arm to near the face obscuring view. Tang Sau arm to high and vulnerable to Tut Sau counters.

2. Bong Sau too low. Overlapping the Fok Sau may lead to trapping and Lop Dar counters.

1. Tang Sau too low may lead to Gum Dar counters.

2. Bong Sau too high wasting unneccesary energy and exposing the mid section.

# PART 5
## BLOCKS & STRIKES

# Blocks (solo)

**Tang Sau -** (outer forearm)

The arm is projected forward in a
deflective manner the fingers can
also double up as a strike to the eyes
or throat.

**Gum Sau -** (palm)

The hand is used to seal an
opponent's attack causing a trapping
or jamming action to occur.

**Wu Sau -** (edge of hand)

This ia a very subtle motion utilising a short wrist manoeuvre to connect the energy force.

**Bong Sau -** (outer forearm)

The arm is projected forward in a corkscrew fashion and can be used as a receiving / yielding block or an offensive / disruptive block.

**Lop Sau -** (fingers & thumb)

This is used to secure and control an opponent's arm. It is also used to redirect or guide an attack.

**Garn Sau -** (outer forearm)

The arm is used in a crude battering fashion maiming the opponent's attacking limb.

**Jum Sau -** (palm/under forearm)

The arm employs a tactile like sliding motion to control and redirect an attack.

**Jau Sau-**(fingers & thumb)

This is a destructive controlling action used to seize an attacker's limb.

**Jut Sau -** (inner forearm)

This is used in an aggressive chopping manner to cause maximum damage to your opponent's limb.

**Biu Sau -** (outer forearm)

The arm is projected forward in a deflective manner the fingers can also double up as a strike to the throat or eyes.

**Tok Sau -** (palm)

This is used in upward / outward action to control and disrupt an opponent's positioning.

# Blocks (applied)

Practice passing these blocks back and forth to each other in a sticking mode.

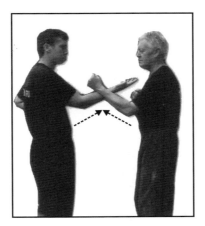

**Tang Sau** - Palm up Arm

Partner A cancels Partner B's strike with a semi-circular forward projection arm spreading action.

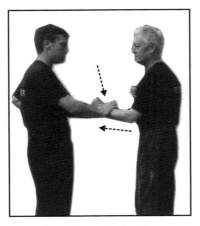

**Gum Sau** - Pinning Arm

Partner A presses the arm of Partner B in a downward fashion to nulify the attack

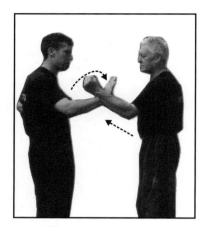

**Wu Sau** - Praying Hand
Using the edge of the hand Partner A redirects for Partner B's punch.

**Bong Sau** - Wing Arm

Partner A intercepts Partner B's
attack by using a corkscrew motion.

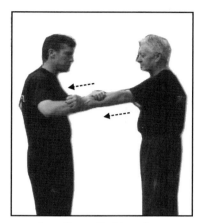

**Lop Sau** - Grabbing Arm

Partner A yanks the forearm of
Partner B directing him away from
the centreline area. (Possible
dislocation).

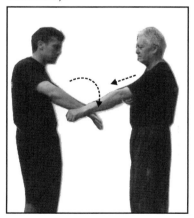

**Garn Sau** - Cultivating Arm

Partner A employs a sweeping
motion to clear Partner B's arm
away from the centreline. (Possible
breakage / fracture).

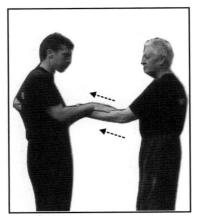

**Jum Sau** - Sinking Arm

Partner A traces Partner B's punch
inward in a controlling manner.

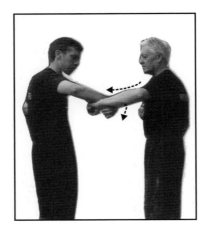

**Kau Sau** - Scooping Arm

Partner A directs Partner B's punch
clear away from the centreline.

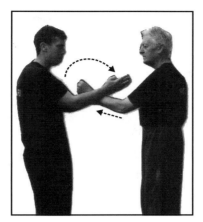

**Jut Sau** - Jerking Arm

Partner A chops downward to intercept Partner B's arm. (Possible breakage / fracture).

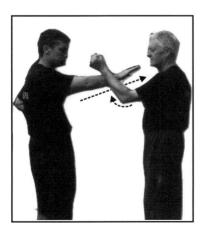

**Biu Sau** - Darting Arm

Partner A uses a spear like action to direct Partner B off the centreline.

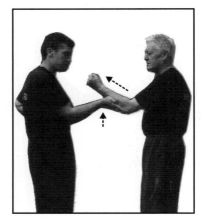

**Tok Sau** - Lifting Arm

Partner A disrupts the stance of
Partner B by using a forward /
upward motion.

**Fok Sau** - Controlling Arm

Partner A uses a hooking manoeuvre
to control Partner B's arm.

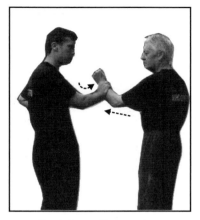

**Paak Sau** - Slapping Arm

Partner A slaps Partner B's arm away
from the centreline area and
disrupting balance.

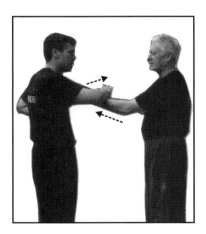

**Lan Sau** - Barring Arm

Partner A uses the underside of the
arm to intercept Partner B's punch.

# Strikes (solo)

**Sau Do** (side of hand)
The arm is thrust outwards in a shovel like action to the opponent's neck / nose / cheek bone / floating ribs or kidney area.

**Chan Sau** (side of hand)
The arm is thrust outwards in a hacking motion to the neck / nose / cheekbone / floating ribs or kidney area.

**Dai Juerng** (palm heel)
This is used to the solar plexus /
stomach and lower abdomen or
groin of the attacker

**Biu Jee** (fingertips)
The hand is employed in a spear like
action to the opponent's eyes or
throat.

**Suerng Jee** (index and middle fingers)
The fingers are used with pin point
accuracy to the underside of earlobe /
eyes / neck and various other pressure
points.

**Chang Choi** (knuckles)
This utilises the fist in a shovel like
action to the opponents solar plexus /
lower abdomen / floating ribs or
kidney area.

**Guerng Jee Choi** (side palm heel)
The hand is employed in a whip like
fashion to smash an attacker's nose /
cheekbone or temple.

**Charp Choi** (index finger knuckle)
The protruding knuckle is used with
pin point accuracy to the underside
of earlobe / temple and floating ribs.

**Fu Jow** (fingertips)
This clawing motion can be used savagely to rip an attacker's face / throat or groin area.

**Pai Jang** (elbow/upper forearm)
Both elbow stump and forearm are used to crudely batter the opponent's temple / cheekbone / nose / chin / jaw / sternum / solar plexus and floating ribs

**Chare Pai Jang** (elbow/upper forearm)
The elbow stump and forearm are used
in a downward motion causing maximum
damage to an attacker's temple / nose /
cheekbone / jaw / sternum / solar plexus
and floating ribs.

# Strikes (applied)

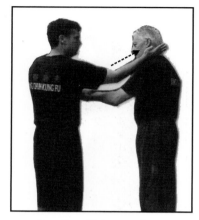

**Sau Do - Palm up Chop**
(side of neck)
Partner A hacks at Partner B's neck
concussing or even maiming him.

**Chan Sau - Chop**
(throat)
Partner A thrusts out a lethal chop
to the windpipe maiming Partner B.

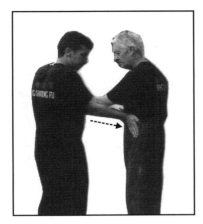

**Dai Juerng - Downward Palm**
(bladder)

Partner A sinks in a low line palm to Partner B's lower abdomen maiming him.

**Biu Do - Ridge Hand**
(side of neck)

Partner A uses a whipping action to concuss or even maim Partner B.

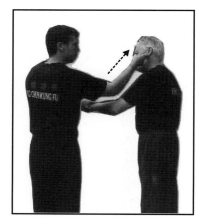

**Suerng Jee - Double Finger**
(under earlobe)

Partner A nails Partner B's pressure point disorientating / concussing or maiming him.

**Wang Juerng - Side Palm**
(chin)

Partner A uses an upward motion to cause disorientation or concussion to Partner B.

**Guerng Jee Choi - Ginger Shape Fist**
(temple)

Partner A employs a whip like action
bringing disorientation / concussion or
even maiming Partner B.

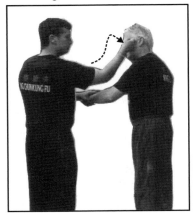

**Charp Choi - (Pheonix) Piercing Punch**
(temple)

Partner A nails Partner B's pressure point
causing disoreintation / concussion or even
maiming him.

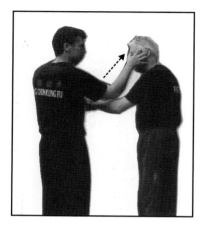

**Fu Jow - Tiger Claw**
(eyes/side of face)

Partner A employs a raking motion
tearing the skin and gouging the eye
of Partner B.

**Pai Jang - Hacking Elbow**
(jaw)

Partner A batters Partner B with an
elbow breaking his jaw and
concussing.

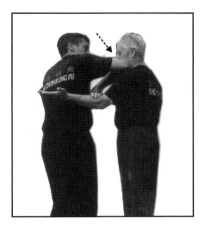

**Chare Pai Jang - Diagonal Hacking Elbow**
(jaw)

Partner A uses a downward elbow motion to
break the jaw and concussing Partner B.

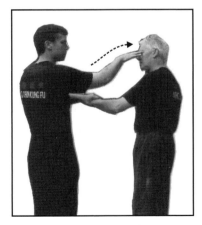

**Biu Jee - Finger Thrust**
(eyes/throat)

Partner A utilises a spearlike action
blinding and disorientating Partner B.

# PART 6
## KICKS & FOOTWORK

# Footwork & Kicking

The footwork and kicking actions in Wing Chun are short but very sweet indeed. There's no jumping spinning kicks, nor is there any elaborate footwork, everything is purely functional with no fancy movements.

Tips:

☐ Keep any footwork whether forward, backward or circular, short, tight, and nimble. Not large strides!

☐ Improve your balance thoroughly with repetitive practice.

☐ Exhale sharply out of the mouth to add extra power to your kicks.

☐ Do not retract kicks afterwards, this will only waste time.

☐ Stamp your foot down fast once a kick is executed.

☐ When you want to kick someone in the groin look at them in the eyes or over their shoulder.

☐ If someone catches your kick spit in their face.

# Kicking at a Distance

When fighting at a distance the practitioner will use plenty of footwork to move both in or / and out of striking range.

Aside from covering the upper torso with the arms it is equally important that you cover your groin with the knee.

This is also applicable when using a short weapon like butterfly knives against a longer weapon such as a pole or spear, the knee is employed to shield the groin area.

# Impact Practice for Kicks

As with all fighting arts you need to get plenty of impact related practice. The beauty of using the Wooden Dummy to develop your kicks is that you can use as much or as little force as you wish, also you can work at various angles.

Here you can see that the kick can double up as a block or strike to mid section limb of the dummy.

The leg of the dummy can be used to represent your opponent's knee or shin. You don't have to kick hard, rather use it as an obstruction.

The inside or outside of your foot can be employed as an imaginary leg sweep. Again accuracy will be better than brute force.

# Kicking Strategies

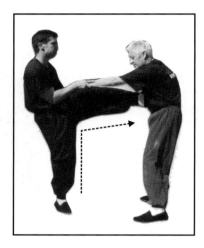

1. Ding Gerk combined with Lop Sau. Kick to the mid section Solar plexus to cause concussion.

2. Dai Wang Dang Gerk combined with Suerng Lop Sau. Kick to the opponent's outer or inner kneecap causing dislocation.

Here are three potential scenarios for applying the Lifting Kick.

1. Upon the opponent seizing the wrist, the defender pulls the arm inwards and combines a Hay Gerk to the lower abdomen.

2. The opponent's punch is countered by using the upper forearm Lan Sau combined with a Hay Gerk.

3. The opponent's punch is countered by using the underside of the forearm, Lan Sau combined with a Hay Gerk.

# Rooting & Uprooting

After absorbing the all important rolling cycles and switching and changing framework we start to address the legs. The introduction of footwork like everything else must be methodical.

The student needs to have a strong "Yee Jee Kum Yueng Ma" or Goat Clamping Stance that can not be easily disrupted. The well rooted stance but also be very ready to shift either forwards, backwards or sidewards.

# Pulling & Pushing

Yet again this relates to the concept of Yin & Yang (negative/positive), in that you are constantly working between the two pulling and pushing forces when engaged in sticking arms training.

The two way push and pull action tests mainly three important areas of both practitioner and opponent.

>   a) The strength and stability of the neutral stance.
>   b) The ability to adjust the footwork upon disruption.
>   c) The stability of the upper torso and particularly the bridges (or forearms).

Standing one's ground is good, but if you have to move then move! Try to go with the strength and not against it, this is the whole purpose of Wing Chun and in fact most martial arts. If a stronger opponent uses a let's say, Lop Dar (grabbing arm with strike) against the weaker opponent, the best action would be to shuffle forward using a defence and attack when being pulled in. Another example of moving with momentum would be let's say the attacker uses a forward step combined with Paak Dar (slapping arm with strike), your response might be to shuffle backwards using some kind of defence and attack to nullify the intention. Side stepping or turning would also be viable in this situation.

# Sticking Legs

Chi Gerk - Sticking Legs is a two man drill which is sometimes incorporated into the practice of Mook Yan Jong - "Wooden dummy" form has been learned. The concept behind the exercises is to gain leg proficiency in kicking, obstructing, trapping, pinning, jamming, sweeping and tripping.

The leg of the Wooden Dummy can form a basis or foundation for solo practice. As with the Double Sticking Arms the Chi Gerk training requires selective movements to be practiced only to be later abandoned into free flow. The principles of contact reflex and sensitivity within the Chi Sau are applied to the Sticking Legs. With practice the student can gain superior balance and single leg dexterity.

# PART 7
## COUNTER ATTACK DRILLS

# Sticking Arm Applications

*Here are some examples of how to use counter-attack applications within Sticking Arms practice.*

1. From a rolling situation Partner A pauses in a Bong Sau / Fok Sau position

2. Immediately a Suerng Tok Sau is made disturbing Partner B's stance.

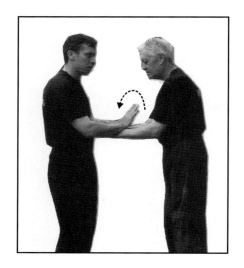

3. Followed by a Suerng Jum Sau to draw in Partner B to the next movement.

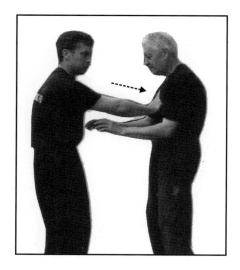

4. Partner B is then repelled by a Suerng Juerng sending him reeling backwards.

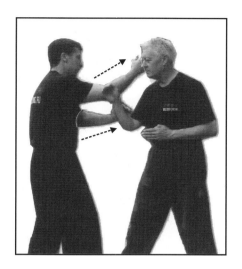

5. Then with a forward step a Paak Dar is delivered drawing Partner B back into the danger zone.

6. Partner B counters with a Paak Sau cancelling the Partner A's potential attack.

7. Partner A seizes the arm with a Lop Dar motion trapping with counter attack.

8. Followed by a Gum Dar immediately to flood Partner B.

9. Resume the rolling situation several times. Partner A pauses in Bong Sau / Fok Sau.

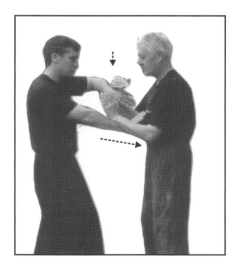

10. Partner A pauses to deliver a Juerng while Partner B counters with Wu Sau to nulify the attack.

11. Partner A steps inward with a Lop Dar using a Jan motion to the solar plexus of Partner B.

12. From there a Kau Dar using a Charp Choi to the floating ribs area of Partner B.

13. This is a immediately followed by a Juerng employing inch force power.

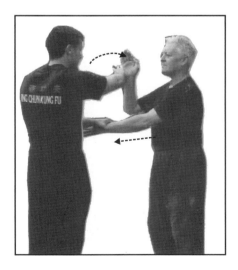

14. The Juerng is then changed to Lop Dar using a Chan Sau, Partner B counters with Wu Sau to stop the attack.

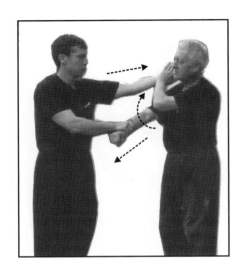

15. Partner A seizes the wrist with Lop Dar using Sau Do. Partner B responds with Paak Sau.

16. Partner A jams with Gum Dar using Pin Jan to jaw area of Partner B.

17. Partner A pulls the arm down to Dai Lop Dar using Chan Sau sealing Partner B's arms.

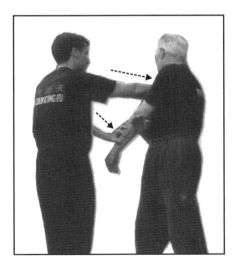

18. Then switches arms to Gum Dar while applying a shoulder shove to disrupt Partner B's posture.

19. From there the rolling situation is resumed again several times.

20. Partner B initiates an outside Tang Sau feed to Partner A's lower Fok Sau position.

21. Partner A employs a Lau Sau using Dai Juerng to the lower abdomen while Partner B cancels it with a Wu Sau.

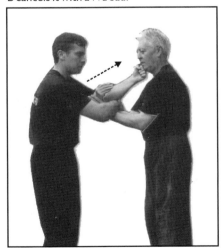

22. Immediately followed with a Lan Sau trap over the top by Partner A to Partner B's arms.

23. From there a Lop Dar is employed using a Chung Choi. Partner B counters with Tang Sau.

24. Followed by a final Paak Dar. Partner B counters with Paak Sau to stop the oncoming attack.
Now return to the double rolling arms several times, alternating the attack and defence scenario between Partner B and Partner A.

# Bong Sau / Lop Dar Cycles

      This is classified as an intermediate training exercise of which there are numerous variations. The initial drill consists of two motions namely the "Bong Sau" - Wing Arm (Yin property) which is used as a defence against the opponents "Lop Dar" - Grab & strike (Yang property) attack. These two actions are passed to and from the opponents using the continuous sticking and forward pressure. As the practitioner gains experience they integrate the Bong Sau / Lop Dar cycles into their rolling arms practice.

Tips:  1. Work at chest height.

          2. Turn with each other in unison.

          3. Keep forward energy.

          4. Cock the fist slightly to make a wedge.

          5. Maintain Sticking mode throughout.

          6. Use pauses in between.

# Preparation (solo)

Left Bong Sau &
Right Wu Sau

Right Lop Sau &
Left Chung Choi

Return to left Bong Sau
& Right Wu Sau

Return to right Lop Sau
& left Chung Choi and so
on...

# Bong Sau / Lop Dau (two man)

1. Partner A takes a defensive position to Partner B offensive position at chest height.

2.With a smooth sticking action alternate to vice versa each other's movements.

3. Again switch to mimic your opponent's last motion.

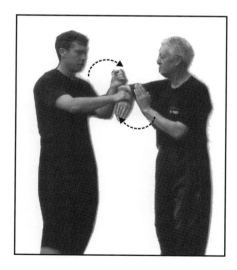

4. Alternate once more before initiating the change.

5. Partner A reaches over to seize Partner B
Wu Sau wrist.

6. Both Partner A and B turn to the other
side and begin again.

7. To break the cycle Partner A cups partner B's elbow sector.

8. Partner B blocks with Gum Sau to Partner A Wang Juerng.

# Gwoh Sau - Crossing Arms

1. Partner A crosses opposite arms with Partner B.

2. Partner A then seizes Partner B's wrist while employing a Ding Sau.

3. Partner A sectors Partner B's wrist.

4. Partner A switches to Gum Dar jamming
Partner B.

5. Partner A immediately traps Partner B with a second Gum Dar.

6. Partner A follows the strike up with Jau Sau throat lock.

# PART 8

# SEARCHING FOR THE BRIDGE
## 2ND FORM

# Chum Kiu
## Searching for the Bridge

The second form in the Wing Chun system is referred to as Chum Kiu and can be translated as meaning "Searching for the Bridge" or "Bridge Seeking". As with the first form Siu Nim Tau it should be taught slowly, section by section. Each movement must be correct before the next is introduced. Where as the first form is performed exclusively in the Goat Clamping Stance the second form utilises footwork, kicks and turning motions. The form traditionally follows after the Double Sticking Arms phase has been thoroughly absorbed.

Although the Chum Kiu (as with all of the forms) can differ from school to school the principles however should remain the same, namely; the Juen Ging - Turning Power to generate striking force and cultivate correct body alignment. The Suerng Lan Sau - Double Barring Arm motions can represent elbow attacks and the Jip Sau - folding Arms can be interpreted as arm breaking combinations. Defensive motions such as the Bong Sau - Wing Arm are a traditional White Crane movement and can be considered for their deflective purposes and also applied into the Bong Sau / Lop Dar sequence drills. Also prevalent are the three types of kicks, those being Hay Gerk - Lifting Kick, Ding Gerk - Nailing Kick and Wang Dang Gerk - Side Nailing Kick.

Here are some important points to consider when practicing the Chum Kiu.

1. Move the body as one unit making sure the shoulders, hips and knees stay flush.
2. Keep any stepping movements to a short tight shuffle. Lead foot first followed by the rear foot.
3. Except when kicking keep your feet flat on the floor and do not favour lifting the heels or toes, especially when turning or twisting
4. Maintain the same pace throughout the entire form. No speeding up or slowing down.
5. Do the actual movements quickly and dynamically but be sure to leave a small pause of one or two seconds between each motion.
6. On completion of any kick stamp the foot down on the floor immediately.

# Section 1

1. Starting with a neutral base Yee Jee Kum Yueng Ma - Goat Clamping Stance.

2. Thrust hands down to make a cross shape with the left arm folded on top of the right arm while pressing together firmly.

3. Without separating the arms, raise up to make a cross shape near the face right arm folded over the top of the left arm this time while pressing together firmly.

4. Draw both fists back sharply.

5. Thrust a left Noy Chung Choi - Inside Punch at shoulder height.

6. Keeping the elbow locked straight, open hand and turn palm face up.

7a. Bunch all fingers together to touch thumb. Bend the wrist up as far as possible.

7b. Keeping the wrist bent back turn hand slowly and smoothly so the fingers and thumb point downward to complete a left Huen Sau - Circling Hand.

8. Form a fist.

9. Draw the left fist back sharply.

10. Thrust a right Noy Chung Choi out at shoulder height.

11. Keeping the elbow locked straight open the hand and turn palm face up.

12a. Bunch all fingers together to touch thumb. Bend wrist upwards as far as possible.

12b. Keeping the wrist bent, turn hand slowlyand smoothly so the fingers point downward to complete a right Huen Sau.

13. Form a fist.

14. Draw the right arm back sharply.

# Section 2

1a. Place both hands in front of chest with wrists cocked and palms facing inwards with a small gap to form a Suerng Ding Sau - Double Retaining Arms.

1b. Complete the Seurng Ding Sau motion by thrusting both the hands until arms lock straight at shoulder height.

2. Angle the right arm underneath and the left arm on, separated slightly at nipple height to form a Suerng Lan Sau - Double Barring Arm. Twist sharply to the left hand side.

3. While maintaining the same arm positioning twist sharply to the right handside.

4. Once again twist sharply back to the left handside.

5. With a scissor like motion thrust both arms out until elbow locks straight with palms facing out at shoulder height.

6. Turn the left arm to a Tang Sau - Palm Up arm position while simultaneously sliding the right palm downward from wrist to elbow completing the first Jip Sau - Folding Arm motion.

7. Turn the right arm to a Tang Sau position while simultaneously sliding the left palm downward from wrist to elbow forming the second Jip Sau motion.

8. Turn the left arm to a Tang Sau position while simultaneously sliding the right palm downward from wrist to elbow forming a third and final Jip Sau.

9. Thrust out a right straight Juerng - Palm at shoulder height while retracting the left hand in a semi-circular fashion.

10. Now thrust out a second straight Juerng while retracting the right hand as before.

11. Once again thrust out a third and final Juerng while retracting the left hand.

12a. Draw the left fist and raise the right arm at nipple height to form a Lan Sau - Barring Arm while twisting sharply to the righthand side

12b. Without moving the Lan Sau rest the left arm on top in Tang Sau position.

12c. Angle the right arm to a Bong Sau - Wing Arm and adjust the left to a Wu Sau - Praying Arm position.

13a. Draw the left fist and raise the right arm at nipple height to form a Lan Sau while twisting sharply to the right hand side again.

13b. Without moving the Lan Sau rest the left arm on top in Tang Sau position.

13c. Angle the right arm to a Bong Sau and adjust the left to a Wu Sau for the second time.

14a. Draw the left fist and raise the left arm at nipple height to form a Lan Sa while twisting sharply to right hand side once more.

14b. Without moving the Lan Sau rest the left arm on top in Tang Sau position.

14c. Angle the right arm to a Bong Sau and adjust the left to a Wu Sau for the third and final time.

15. Retract the right arm while immediately executing a left Noy Chung Choi.

16. Adjust the right foot inward to return to the neutral stance combining a Fak Sau - Whisking Arm at shoulder height to the left hand side.

17. Using an arc like shape movement change the arm to a Wu Sau position.

18a. Turn the right Wu Sau into a Tang Sau position while resting the left hand palm up on the inner forearm. Ready to make Tut Sau - Freeing Arm.

18b. Thrust the right arm downwards while sliding the left hand on inner forearm. Then immediately both vice versa at wrist level.

18c. Draw the right hand sharply down while locking the left arm straight to complete the Tut Sau motion.

19. Draw the left arm back sharply.

20. Bend the wrist inward and rotate the hand slowly and smoothly to complete a left Huen Sau.

NOW COMPLETE THE ENTIRE SEQUENCE OF SECTION 2 ON THE OTHER HAND SIDE

# Section 3

1. Turn to the left while combining a closed fisted left Lan Sau and Hay Gerk - Lifting Kick.

2. Immediately finish the kick with a stamp. Maintain the upper body positioning.

3a. Side step to the left hand side raise a left Bong Sau with a right Wu Sau.

3b. Retract both elbows inwards, left arm overlapping the right with palms facing pwards.

4a. Side step to the left hand side and raise a second left Bong Sau and a right Wu Sau.

4b. Retract both elbows inwards left arm overlapping the right with palms facing upwards.

5. Side step to the left hand side and raise a left Bong Sau and a right Wu Sau for the third and final time.

6. Immediately turn the left hand side while drawing the left hand to a fist and thrusting out a Pau Choi - Cannon Punch.

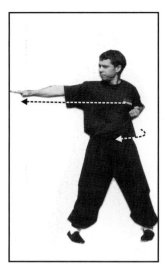

7. Turn the right foot inward to return to the neutral stance thrusting out a Fak Sau at shoulder height to the left hand side.

8. Using an arc like shape move the arm to a Wu Sau position.

9a. Turn the right Wu Sau into a Tang Sau position while resting the left hand palm up on the inner forearm ready to make a Tut Sau.

9b. Thrust the right arm downwards while sliding the left hand along inner forearm. Then immediately turn both vice versa at wrist level.

124

9c. Draw the right arm sharply while locking the left arm straight to complete the Tut Sau motion.

10. Bend the wrist inwards and rotate the hand slowly and smoothly to complete a left Huen Sau.

11. Form a fist.

12. Draw the left arm sharply.

NOW COMPLETE THE ENTIRE SEQUENCE OF SECTION 3 ON THE OTHER HAND SIDE

125

# Section 4

1. Turn to the left hand side while executing a Ding Gerk - Nailing Kick.

2. Immediately finish the kick with a stamp.

3a. Move forward with the lead leg combined with a Suerng Dai Bong - Double Low Wing Arm position.

3b. Retract both elbows inwards to make a Suerng Tang Sau - Double Palm Up Arm position.

4a. Once again move forward while combining a Suerng Dai Bong Sau.

4b. Retract both elbows inwards to make a Suerng Tang Sau.

5. Move forward while combining a Suerng Dai Bong Sau for the third time.

6. Move the rear foot forward to meet the lead foot. Keep the knees bent and thrust out a Suerng Juerng - Double Palm strike.

7a. Keeping the elbows locked straight drop both arms downwards and bend the wrists.

7b. Rotate the arms inwards wrists pressing together.

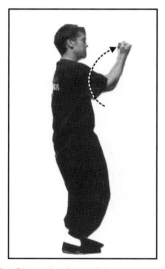

7c. Close the fists while continuing the rotation to form a Suerng Fon Choi - Double Back Fist motion.

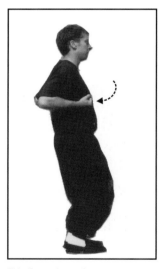

7d. Complete the movements by drawing both fists to the side smoothly.

NOW COMPLETE THE ENTIRE SEQUENCE OF SECTION 4 ON THE OTHER HAND SIDE

# Section 5

1. Turn to the left hand side and execute a left Wang Dang Gerk - Side Nailing Kick.

2. Stamp the left foot downwards and combine a right Gum Sau - Pinning Arm.

3. Follow this with a Chung Choi using the same arm.

4. Turn to the right hand side combining a left Gum Sau.

5. Follow this with a Chung Choi with the same arm.

6. Turn to left hand side while executing a right Gum Sau and a left Wu Sau.

7. Turn to the right hand side while executing a left Gum Sau and a right Wu Sau.

8. Turn to the left hand side while executing a right Gum Sau and a Wu Sau.

9. Angle the right foot inward to secure the neutral Yee Jee Kum Yuerng Ma and thrust out a left Lien Wan Choi - Centre Punch.

10. Thrust out a right Lien Wan Choi.

11. Thrust out a final left Lien Wan Choi.

12. Draw both arms sharply.

13. With a sliding motion retract your right leg inwards to meet the left leg.

Note: THE FORM IS COMPLETE DO NOT REPEAT SECTION 5 ON THE OTHER SIDE

# Folding Arm Keys

Connect the following motions together smoothly , sliding along the inner forearm.

1a. Cock the palm with heel resting on the Tang Sau position.

1b. As you move downwards lay the whole palm on the arm.

1c. Continue with the motion until the palm meets the elbow.

2. Change to repeat the same on the other side.

# Palm Striking Keys

Connect the following motions together smoothly , sliding along the underside of the forearm this time.

1a. From the last palm strike.

2a. Begin the next palm straighten the last one and moving gradually inwards.

2b. Continue sliding the back of the hand under the arm.

2c. Turn the hand to Wu Sau at the elbow point cocking the palm heel backwards.

# PART 9
# FIGHTING APPLICATIONS

# Fighting Applications

There are no specific quantity or order for Chum Kiu related fighting applications. They are countless and unpredictable as once you have absorbed the principles everything should just become automatic. Think of it like this....when the opponent initiates an attack he / she will only end up hurting themselves. The more vicious their assault the more danger they will be enveloping themselves in. Your reaction should be totally non premeditated to the point of being almost accidental.

By now your hands and arms should be well conditioned through wallbag and two man arm toughening exercises. This will mean all your blocks and strikes will be heavy, effortless and damaging to your enemy. Also your sensitivity and reaction reflex levels should be very acute thanks to all Sticking Arms practice, this too will greatly work to your advantage, thus heightening your chances of winning.

Here are some random examples of Chum Kiu fighting applications.

1a) The attacker steps in with a right hooking punch. The defender responds with a Jum Sau - Sticking Arm (shock no. 1) destroying the bicep and joint area.

1b) The defender immediately switches to a Jip Sau - fold over arm (shock no. 2) causing dislocation or breakage.

2a) The attacker then throws a left hooking punch. The defender blocks with a left Chuen Sau - threading block while controlling the attacker's original arm.

2b) The defender switches to a Pong Geng Sau - neck pulling arm combined with a "Goats head" smash to the attacker's nose.

1a) The attacker initiates a right shoulder grab. The defender re-directs their forearm.

1b) The defender controls the range by the gap and applying a Tarn Dar - bounce off arm and strike using a Biu Do - ridge hand (shock no. 1) to the attacker's neck.

2a) The attacker then throws a left straight punch while the defender counter attacks with Paak Dar - slapping arm & strike using a low Chan Sau - chop to the floating ribs (shock no.2)

2b) This is immediately followed by a final devastating chop to the attacker's neck.

a) The attacker reaches out to grab the defender around the throat with the right arm

b) The defender immediately breaks out by controlling the hand while applying a Jut Sau - jerking arm (shock no.1) to the attacker's inner forearm causing nerve destruction.

c) The defender folds then peels back quickly the attacker's arm with a Kau Dar - scooping arm & strike using a Juerng - palm (shock no.2) to the forehead.

d) This is immediately followed by a foot trip taking the attacker to the floor (shock no.3) and breaking his arm.

143

1a) The attacker throws a right hooking punch. The defender responds with a Jum Sau - sinking arm (shock no. 1) and Tong Gerk - stomp kick on the shin.

1b) With one smooth action the defender moves to outside using a Huen Sau - circling then Suerng Wu Sau - double praying arm (shock no. 2) causing dislocation or breakage.

2a) The attacker desparately throws a left hooking punch which the defender intercepts with a second double arm break (shock no.3)

2b) This is immediately followed by a foot sweep taking the attacker to the floor.

# Practicality

Using practical solutions to counter attack your opponent is vital, it doesn't matter if you're in a Sticking Arm situation or being attacked on the street. React with the simplist, most effective auto response you can, it's not rocket science so use the economy of motion!

The very moment your opponent initiates an attack by aggressively grabbing your arm..

Respond with a swift punch on the chin. No wrist locks, no tie ups, no aggro required.

# PART 10
## ADVANCED KNOWLEDGE

# The Higher Levels

Once you know the principles of "Sticking" you can stick arms, legs, wooden dummies, poles etc. There are various degrees of advanced Sticking Arms practice that require a great deal of concentration. I would not recommend the practice I am describing with the following training drills without some kind of third (or even fourth) party of supervision as things could get very dangerous.

Here are some variations of advanced Sticking Arms:

"**BLINDFOLDED STICKING ARMS**" is where one of the practitioners utilises the total feeling and vibration his opponent is giving him by way of covering his ability to see what's occurring.

"**PLUM BLOSSOM STICKING ARMS**" is where both practitioners perform their training on a raised platform (such as a table) or for very advanced practitioners on top of large wooden stakes erected into the ground at levels or spaces apart. This kind of training emphasises superior footwork.

"**THREE MAN STICKING ARMS**" is where three (or more) practitioners engage in rolling, switching and drilling their techniques as one unit. The good behind this exercise is to heighten the co-ordination.

*Author's note: My former Wing Chun Sifu actually practiced the "Three Man Sticking Arms" with Wong Shun Lueng and Bruce Lee no less!*

# Sticking Pole

In the latter stages of the Wing Chun system we incorporate the principles of the Sticking Arms into the Chi Gwan - Sticking Pole practice.

The basic concept is much the same in the fact that the two practitioners use the Yin / Yang cycles between various attack and defense motions.

# Competing

Some practitioners like to enter Chi Sau competitions as this is seen as a good way to pressure test what has been learnt. Unfortunately some of the reality can be lost with the protective clothing which although necessary for safety can however restrict movement and flow. This doesn't stop these competitions from having their share of injured opponents as they can get quite savage!

Chi Sau tournaments are all over the world. Some endorse light or semi-contact, others use full-contact (even without protective gear!). Some use weight categories, while others use grades or ages. The prizes can range from trophies, medals, money or simply prestige. One of the 'Creme de la Creme' of the Chi Sau contests are held in Hong Kong and Macau.

Another fairly recent method of competing is by taking part in a "continuous Chi Sau Marathon". These are usually conducted over several hours in aid of raising money for charity.

# Chi Sau Games

Here are two Chi Sau exercises that will help to improve upper body positioning and balance.

1. Practice Sticking Arms while both you and your opponent are sitting opposite to each other.

2. Practice Sticking Arms while both you and your opponent are standing on one leg with your knee to the outside.

# After Thoughts

Wing    Chun is considered to be a way of life rather than a competitive sport. I love philosophy I find it can help to make us grow spiritually. There are numerous Wing Chun sayings and proverbs, but since they have been quoted endlessly before in other books I won't include any of them here. The following words of wisdom have been around for hundreds, even thousands of years and are applicable to our everyday lives in general.

If we only practice the aggressive attributes (Yang Properties) we will produce an imbalance both in martial art training and everyday lives. The sayings are powerful codes that help us to look deep inside ourselves for their positive meanings. A greater study of the spiritual aspects will be addressed in the forth book of the series "Darting Fingers hidden form of Wing Chun".

Now take your time to ponder these thoughts:

"The contented man, even though poor is happy;
    The discontented man, even though rich is sad.."

"Do not be concerned about others not appreciating you,
    Be concerned about you not appreciating others..."

"Don't show your poem to a fencing master, show it to a poet..."

"Do not fear going forward slowly; fear only to stand still..."

"It is not the movement; it is the idea behind the movement..."

"Many blossoms and few fruits, that is the work of heaven;
    many words and few deeds, that is the fault of man..."

"Simplicity is the last step of art, and the beginning of nature..."

"It's not how much you know, it's how much you understand..."

"If you think you know already, then you can never learn!"

"Be soft yet not weak; be firm but yet not hard..."

"There are two sides to a coin, never judge a book by its' cover..."

"Listen to both sides and you will be enlightened,
        hear only one side and you will be benighted..."

"Sow a thought and you reap an act,
    Sow an act and you reap a habit,
    Sow a habit and you reap a character,
     Sow a character and you reap a destiny..."

# Afterword

Wing Chun is quite different these days, many schools teach their syllabus very quickly in fact there are even places and website home study courses that offer to make people branch instructors in a very short time indeed. There is often confusion in the concept that the more forms you learn the more knowledgeable you will become, but more forms does not mean more skill! Anyone can pick up a book, video or dvd and copy the movements on them. The real proof is in the pudding or in other words the practitioners Chi Sau abilities.

Many students are taught Sticking Arms within a period of months (or even weeks I've heard!). I am not condoning this as it is down to how much time and effort has been put in but problems can arise when they stick arms with a practitioner who spent great lengths of time getting their basics right and the principles fully absorbed. Those who have been taught gradually and to analyse can feel the quality or level of the opponent just by rolling with no need for giving or receiving any attacks.

A good Sifu / instructor will guide you the student slowly piece by piece over a period of years (yes years!). Sometimes a student might not learn anything new for several months and the reason for this could be three fold i.e; 1) Because the technique being drilled might not be deemed as being fully correct. 2) The teacher is holding back the student to instil the true Taoist method of patience and perseverance to lead the student into the transitional reality theory of 'letting go'. 3) To cultivate the internal energies within the Sticking Arms practice.

What I've outlined in this book as I mentioned earlier are the fundamentals and now it is up to you to ingrain them into yourself through much hands on practice.

My next book will continue from where we left off addressing the next important stepping stone to the Wing Chun system. The book is to be entitled "Wing Chun Wooden Dummy - dynamic training methods". It will cover; how to make a wooden dummy on a budget, hand and foot positioning, sticking flow drills, the entire Wooden Dummy form and how the form can be broken down into potent fighting applications.

# Terminology
### (in Cantonese dialect)

**Baat Jam Dau** - Eight Slash Knives

**Bik Ging** - Pressing Force

**Bik Ma** - Pressing Stance

**Biu Do** - Ridge Hand

**Biu Jee/Tze** - Darting Fingers

**Bong Sau** - Wing Arm

**Chare Pai Jang** - Diagonal Hacking Elbow

**Charp Choi** - Piercing Punch

**Chan Sau** - Chopping Hand

**Chi** - Sticking and Life Force

**Chi Sau** - Sticking Arms

**Choi** - Punch

**Chum Kiu** - Searching for the Bridge

**Gung Fu** - Skill Effect

**Dan Chi Sau** - Single Sticking Arm

**Dai** - Low

**Ding Gerk** - Nailing kick

**Ding Sau** - Nailing Hand

**Fak Sau** - Whisking Arm

**Fok Sau** - Controlling Arm

**Hay Gerk** - Lifting Kick

**Huen Sau** - Circling Hand

**Garn Sau** - Cultivating Arm

**Gerk** - Kick

**Ging** - Power or Force

**Guerng Jee Choi** - Ginger Shape Fist

**Gum Gok Ging** - Sensitivity & Reaction

**Gum Sau** - Pinning Hand

**Gung Lik** - Building Energies

**Gwoh Sau** - Crossing Arms

**Jang** - Elbow

**Jau Sau** - Clawing Hand

**Jee/Tze** - Fingers

**Jip Sau** - Folding Arm

**Joon Seen** - Centreline

**Juen** - Turn

**Juen Ma** - Turning Stance

**Juerng** - Palm

**Jum Sau** - Sinking Arm

**Jut Sau** - Jerking Arm

**Kam Sau** - Binding Arm

**Kau Sau** - Scooping Arm

**Kuen** - Fist

**Kung Fu** - Westernised term for Gung Fu

**Kwoon** - School (of training)

**Lan Sau** - Barring Arm

**Lau Sau** - Slipping Arm

**Lin Sil Dai Dar** - Simultaneous Attack & Defence

**Lin Wan Choi** - Chain Punching

**Lok Sau** - Rolling Arms

**Lok Ma** - Sitting Stance

**Lop Sau** - Grabbing Arm

**Ma** - Stance

**Mai Jarn** - Immoveable Elbow

**Mook Yan Jong** - Wooden Dummy

**Ngoy** - Outside

**Noy** - Inside

**Paak Sau** - Slapping Hand

**Pai Jang** - Hacking Elbow

**Pau Choi** - Cannon Punch

**Poon Sau** - Rolling Arms

**Pong Geng Sau** - Neck Pulling Grab

**Sibak** - Kung Fu Uncle

**Sifu** - (Kung Fu) Father

**Sigung** - (Kung Fu) Grandfather

**Si hung** - (Kung Fu) Elder Brother

**Sijo** - (Kung Fu) Founder

**Simo** - (Kung Fu) Mother

**Siu Nim Tau** - The Little Idea

**Suerng** - Double

**Tang Sau** - Palm up Arm

**Tok Sau** - Lifting Arm

**Tut Sau** - Freeing Arm

**Ving Tsun** - Yip Man spelling for Wing Chun

**Wang Dang Gerk** - Side Nailing Kick

**Wang Gerg** - Side Kick

**Wang Juerng** - Side Palm

**Wing Chun** - Always Spring

**Wing Tsun** - Modernised term for Wing Chun

**Wu Sau** - Praying Protective Hand

**Yip Man** - The Late Sigung of Wing Chun/Ving Tsun